LET'S TALK ABOUT
GETTING HURT

by Joy Berry • Illustrated by Maggie Smith

Copyright© Joy Berry, 2022
Originally Published, 1995

All rights are reserved.

No part of this book can be duplicated or used without the prior written permission of the copyright owner, except for the use of brief quotations from the book.

For inquiries or permission requests contact the publisher.

Published by Joy Berry Enterprises
www.joyberryenterprises.com

Hello, my name is Chilly.

I live with Tami.

Most of the time, Tami likes to do new things.

When Tami does something for the first time, she sometimes worries about getting hurt.

You might worry about getting hurt when you do something for the first time, too.

You might worry about getting hurt when you do something all by yourself.

You might worry about getting hurt when you do something that's hard to do.

You might worry about getting hurt when you try to do something you don't know how to do.

You might worry about getting hurt when you have to do something you're not big or strong enough to do.

Once in a while, you might find yourself in a position to do something you know could be harmful to you.

Getting hurt is no fun.

But constantly worrying about getting hurt isn't fun, either.

Too much worrying can keep you from trying new, fun things.

Most of the time, you don't need to worry about trying new things.

If you're afraid of getting hurt, talk to an adult about what you want to do.

Usually that person can help you figure out the best way to do it, or tell you if it's too difficult or dangerous.

You shouldn't do anything that could be dangerous unless an adult is nearby to make sure you are safe.

Be sure you know the correct way to do what you want to do.

If needed, ask an adult to teach you how.

When you're doing something new or difficult, go slowly.

Do a little bit at a time.

Before you know it, you'll be ready to do more.

When you're doing something new or difficult, be careful.

Pay close attention to what you are doing.

Concentrating will help you accomplish what you want to do.

Sometimes you might get hurt even though you're going slowly and being careful.

Try not to panic when you get hurt.

Ask an adult to help you.

Tell that person what happened, where it hurts, and how you feel.

Everybody gets hurt once in a while.

But if you go slowly and carefully and get help when you need it, most of the time you can do new things with confidence and have a lot of fun!

Let's talk about... **Joy Berry!**

As the inventor of self-help books for kids, Joy Berry has written over 250 books that teach children about taking responsibility for themselves and their actions. With sales of over 80 million copies, Joy's books have helped millions of parents and their kids.

Through interesting stories that kids can relate to, Joy Berry's Let's Talk About books explain how to handle even the toughest situations and emotions. Written in a clear, simple style and illustrated with bright, humorous pictures, the Let's Talk About books are fun, informative, and they really work!

www.ingramcontent.com/pod-product-compliance
Lightning Source LLC
Chambersburg PA
CBHW081412070526
44583CB00020B/2773